BITS of MOUNTAIN SPEECH

PAUL M. FINK
Jonesboro, Tennessee

The Appalachian Consortium was a non-profit educational organization composed of institutions and agencies located in Southern Appalachia. From 1973 to 2004, its members published pioneering works in Appalachian studies documenting the history and cultural heritage of the region. The Appalachian Consortium Press was the first publisher devoted solely to the region and many of the works it published remain seminal in the field to this day.

With funding from the Andrew W. Mellon Foundation and the National Endowment for the Humanities through the Humanities Open Book Program, Appalachian State University has published new paperback and open access digital editions of works from the Appalachian Consortium Press.

www.collections.library.appstate.edu/appconsortiumbooks

ISBN (pbk.: alk. Paper): 978-1-4696-3819-5
ISBN (ebook): 978-1-4696-3821-8

Distributed by the University of North Carolina Press
www.uncpress.org

BITS OF MOUNTAIN SPEECH

gathered between 1910 and 1965

along the mountains bordering

North Carolina and Tennessee

FOREWORD

BITS OF MOUNTAIN SPEECH

Although Mr. Paul Fink does not profess to be an academician - in fact, in his modesty he would deny it even if we were to insist upon it -, he has achieved a scholarly work in this compilation of folk speech.

What is folk speech, anyway? Briefly, it is the language of what is usually considered the uneducated or less well educated folk; it is sometimes archaic, almost always idiomatic, and it is of course dialectal. Frequently it is quaint; more frequently, it is simply a holdover of vocabulary, pronunciation, and syntax of earlier times when it was accepted as good usage.

In this work Mr. Fink has performed a service for anyone interested in language, speech patterns, and communication. Not only has he listed the unusual words which he himself has heard, but he uses each one in a sentence in order to interpret the work or phrase and to clarify it. Further, he even informs the reader as to the part of speech each word assumes as he lists it.

This book is only one of the many contributions which Mr. Fink has made to a study of the history and lore of East Tennessee and Western North Carolina. Among the earliest to become alert to the significance of the culture and heritage of his native area, he has also been among the most active and enthusiastic proponents of preserving the remaining expressions of the past of his region.

As you read these words and phrases, you will be amused at some, perplexed by some, and entertained by all of them. Some will even make you nostalgic. Reading this book is an interesting and educational experience.

Ambrose N. Manning
Department of English
East Tennessee State University
and
Chairman, Board of Directors
The Appalachian Consortium, Inc.

May 1, 1974

i

All this material was gathered along the Tennessee-North Carolina border, between 1910-1965. During that period there has been much change in the mountain culture and speech. The impact of two world wars, when thousands of young men spent months and years in an environment utterly different from what they had known: compulsory education; good roads; electric power; telephones, radio and TV; public works and the mailorder catalog -- all have wrought great changes in the way of life in the Southern mountains. The mountain people as I first knew them are a vanished breed. And the change has not always been for the better.

The notations in parentheses indicate the parts of speech, i.e., (n)-noun; (v)-verb; (adj)-adjective; (adv)-adverb; (pn)-pronoun; (prep)-preposition; (conj)-conjunction.

A

abide (v): tolerate, endure. *"I can't abide them kind."*

acrost (prep): across. *"They live acrost the river."*

admire to (v): be pleased. *"I'd shorely admire to see him agin."*

afeared (adj): afraid. *"He's afeared o'hants."*

afore (prep): before. *"Git home afore night."*

agin or **aginst** (prep): by the time of. *"I'll be home aginst dark."*

agin (prep): by, against. *"Hits over agin the fence."*

aholt or **holt** (v): hold. *"I took aholt of him."*

aidge (n): edge. *"The tree growed on the aidge of the clift."*

ailing (adj): ill or sick. *"John has been ailing three weeks past."*

aim to (v): intend, plan. *"I aim to go."*

ain't (v): am, is or are not. *"They ain't here yet."*

ain't much (adj): not feeling well. *"John ain't much these days."*

airish (adj): windy, cool. *"Hit's plumb airish out."*

allers (adv): always. *"He's allers late."*

along about sundown (adv): late in the afternoon.

anent or **fernent** (prep): close to or by. *"His house stood anent the church house."*

a-nigh (prep): near. *"I'll shoot if he comes a-nigh me."*

antic (adj): joking, playful. *"He was an antic sort of feller."*

apple-fruit (n): cooked apples. **"Pass the apple fruit."**

argufy (v): to argue. *"They'd argufy all night."*

ary (pn): any. *"Has ary one of you got a match?"*

atter (prep): after. *"They come atter night."*

ax (v): ask. *"You ax him."*

B

back (v): to address a letter. *"Will you **back** this letter for me?"*

bad sick, bad hurt, bad off (adj): in serious condition. *"His woman is bad off."*

bait (n): food, generally a large amount. *"He et a real **bait** o'greens."*

ballet (n): ballad. *"She know a awful lot of old **ballets**."*

banter (v): challenge. *"John **bantered** him for a race."*

basement (n): basin. *"A little **basement** between the hills."*

battling block, battling stick (n): a smooth wooden block on which clothes are beaten with a battling stick while being washed.

beal (v): to fester, as an abscess. *"I had a **bealed** ear."*

bealing (n): a boil or abscess. *"Mary had a **bealing** on her neck."*

beast, beastes (n): horses. *"He had four head o' **beastes**."*

beat or **beat out** (adv): exhausted. *"I'm plumb **beat out**."*

beatinest (adj): superlative adjective. *"They was the **beatinest** crowd at the burying."*

bedevil (v): worry or tease. *"Don't **bedevil** that dog."*

bee-gum (n): beehive, formerly made from a section of a hollow gum log.

beholden (adj): obligated. *"I'm not **beholden** to him."*

benighted (adj): detained after nightfall. *"John figured he'd be home by sundown, but he was **benighted**."*

best (adv): should or had better. *"They **best** go home afore hit rains."*

betwixt (prep): between. *"The house was **betwixt** the hill and the branch."*

biggety (adj): conceited or bigoted. *"She's got no reason to act so **biggety**."*

bigness (n): size. *"A hole the **bigness** of a bullet."*

biscuit bread (n): biscuits.

blackberry winter (n): an unseasonably cool spell of weather in May.

blockage (n): illicit whiskey.

blockading (v) and **blockader** (n): making and maker of illicit whiskey.

2

blow-down (n): area where the timber has been levelled by high wind. *"There's a terrible big blow-down on the far side of the mountain."*

blowed (v): blew. *"He blowed the whistle."*

bodaciously (adv): completely, totally. *"I'm most bodaciously wore out."*

body (n): person. *"Hit won't do a body any good."*

bone tired (adj): very tired.

book-larnin' (n): education derived from books. *"He's short on book-larnin'."*

boughten (adj): purchased, as at a store. *"She was wearing a boughten dress."*

boundary (n): track of land. *"They bought a big boundary of timber."*

branch (n): small stream. *"They are fishing down in the branch."*

bread (v): *"He raised enough corn to bread his family."*

bresh (n): bushes or brush, as growing in an old clearing or woods.

brickle or **brickley** (adj): brittle. *"That bread is awful brickley."*

brigetty or **briggedy** (adj): same as biggety.

broke (v): dismissed. *"Has meeting broke yet?"*

brought-on (adj): from another place. *"They was eating brought-on vittles."*

budget (n): bundle or package. *"His clothes was rolled in a budget."*

burying (n): funeral, particularly the interment. *"Did you stay for the burying?"*

burying ground (n): cemetery or graveyard.

C

call to mind (v): remember. *"I can't call to mind what his name was."*

carry (v): take, accompany. *"I have to carry my woman to the doctor tomorrow."*

catched, cotch, cotched (v): caught.

caucus (v): talk idly. *"They set around an' caucussed all day."*

chance (n): prospect. *"A good chance of corn."*

chancy (adj): doubtful, dangerous. *"Hit was a chancy sort of thing."*

cheese (n): always plural. *"them cheese."*

chimbley (n): chimney.

choicey (adj): particular, fastidious. *"You needn't be so choicey about it."*

choose (v): desire, wish. *"Do you want some fruit? No, I wouldn't choose any."*

choosey (adj): same as choicey.

chuffy (adj): short, stout. *"He's a chuffy sort of boy."*

chunk (v): stir. *"Chunk up the fire."* Also to throw. *"Chunk me the ball."*

church (v): to put on trial before the congregation. *"They churched him for drinking."*

church-house (n): church building.

clever (adj): obliging, good natured. *"He was a mighty clever man."*

clift (n): cliff.

clim or **clum** (v): past tense of climb.

coalin' ground (n): spot where charcoal was made, for early iron furnace.

coal oil (n): kerosene.

come (prep): by or about. *"They'll git here come night."*

come on to rain (v): began. *"I went in the house when it come on to rain."*

come through (v): profess religion. *"Did John come through at the meetin' last night?"*

complected (adj): color of skin. *"He's sorter dark complected."*

contrary (v): oppose. *"Don't contrary him none."*

coon: climb or crawl. *"I cooned up a tree."*

cooter (v): spend time idly. *"He cootered around all day."*

costes (v): costs. *"Hit costes too much."*

course (v): to follow or trail. *"He can course a bee to hit's hive."*

court (v): to sue at law. *"Jones courted Smith over a horse."*

cow brute (n): bull. Sometimes any bovine.

creel (v): to reel, give way or fall. *"His leg creeled under him."*

cresses, creeses (n): water cress or a field salad, always in the plural. Sometimes "creasy-greens."

critter (n): horse or mule, sometimes any kind of animal. *"Wild critters."*

crope (v): crept. *"I crope up on a deer."*

cuckold (v): to be unfaithful maritally. *"Jim's wife cuckolded him."*

cuss-fight (n): interchange of profanity.

D

damn (adj; adv): superlative adjective or adverb. *"The worstest fight I ever damn seen."*

dast (v): dare. *"They don't dast go."*

deadening (n): area where timber had died from disease or killed by girdling, preparatory to clearing. *"Go down to the deadening and git some firewood."*

decoration (n): memorial service held at a rural church, when graves are decorated with flowers. *"When is the decoration at the Bab'tis church?"*

destroyed (v): killed. *"When I heered you'd gone to the war, I was afeared you'd been destroyed."*

devil (v): tease or worry. *"Make him quit devilling the dog."*

dicker (v): discuss, as in a trade. *"They been dickering over that horse for weeks."*

die out (v): die. *"All my chillun died out on me."*

differ (v): make a difference. *"Hit don't differ none which one I get."*

dilitary (adj): slothful, procrastinating. *"He's plumb dilitary."*

dip (v): use snuff. *"Do you dip or chew?"*

discomfit (v): to inconvenience. *"Ef it don't discomfit ye none."*

disregardless (adj): regardless.

disremember (v): forgot. *"I disremember what day it was."*

doctor medicine (n): medicine as prescribed by a doctor and bought at a drug store, as opposed to home remedies.

dodger (n): cornbread baked in a cake or pone.

doesn't differ (v): make any difference. *"Hit doesn't differ which one you take."*

dog irons (n): andirons.

dog trot or **dog alley** (n): open but covered runway between the two parts of a log cabin.

do-less (adj): lazy or trifling. *"I'm feeling plumb do-less this morning."*

doney-gal (n): sweetheart.

doste or **dastes** (n): dose. *"She taken two dostes o' medicine."*

dotey (adj): aged or senile. *"He's got plumb dotey."*

doublings (n): whiskey put through the still twice, to eliminate solid matter and other impurities; a process generally eliminated by the use of a thumping chest or keg.

down (adj): fallen. *"A heap of down timber."*

down-go (adj; n): declining health. *"He's been on the down-go fer sometime."*

draw up (v): shrink. *"My jacket drawed up 'till purt nigh couldn't get hit on."*

dreen (n): drain or gully. *"The fox was runnin' down the dreen."*

dremp (v): dreamed. *"I dremp o' rain last night."*

drug (v): dragged. *"I drug in a lot o' firewood."*

druthers (n): choice. *"If I had my druthers I'd a stayed home."*

dry land sled (n): sled to be used in fields or dirt roads.

dulcimore (n): pronunciation of dulcimer.

E

easing powders (n): drug to ease pain. *"They ought to a' give him some easing powders."*

eats good (v): appetizing. *"Bear meat* **eats good."**

eend (n): end. *"He come to the* **eend** *o' the road."*

effen (conj): if. *"I'll go,* **effen** *ye don't mind."*

enduring (prep): during. *"Did he stay* **enduring** *the night?"*

enty (v): isn't he. **"Enty** *going?"*

'est or **'ist** (adj): just or only. *"They's* **'est** *two o' us."*

et (v): eat or eaten. *"Have ye* **et** *yet?"*

evening (n): afternoon, before night.

eye doctor (n): oculist.

F

fagged out (adj): exhausted. *"I'm plumb **fagged out**."*

fall (v): to chop down. *"We're goin' to have to **fall** that tree."*

fall off (v): lose weight. *"She's **fall off** 20 pound."*

falling weather (n): rainy or snowy weather.

fault (v): to blame or criticize. *"They shouldn't **fault** him over that."*

favor (v): resemble. *"The boy **favors** his daddy."*

feel for (v): incline to. *"I didn't **feel for** to work."*

fernint (prep): near, against. *"Over **fernint** the house."*

fetch (v): bring. *"Be shore to **fetch** some eggs."*

ficsty (adj): pert, impudent. *"She's plumb **ficsty** these days."*

fightin'est (adj): very pugnacious. *"That's the **fightin'est** dog."*

figured (v): thought. *"I **figgered** he'd come next week."*

fireboard (n): mantel or shelf above the fireplace.

fire-dogs (n): andirons or wooden chunks used as such.

fistes (n): fists.

fitten (adj): fit, suitable. *"Hit's a **fitten** name."*

fittified (adj): subject to fits or "spells."

flax (v): hurry. *"I'll **flax** around and git dinner."*

fleshy (adj): fat. *"She's a **fleshy** old woman."*

folkses (n): folks.

follow (v): practice a trade or occupation. *"He **follows** carpenterin'."*

foreigner (n): one living outside the mountains.

for to (adv): *"I didn't mean **for to** do that."*

for why (adv): why. *"I don't rightly know **for why**."*

fotch (v): brought. *"They **fotch** it yesterday."*

fotch-on (adj): imported. *"I don't favor them **fotch-on** ideas."*

frail or **flail** (v): beat, flog. *"I'll most pointedly **frail** hell outen him."*

friz (v): frozen. *"The river was **friz** over solid."*

fruit (n): applies to apples only. *"Have some* **fruit."**

funeralize (v): preach a funeral for.

fur piece (n): long distance. *"Hit's a* **fur piece** *from here."*

fustest (adv): first. *"Who got there* **fustest?"**

G

galack (v): to gather galax or other ornamental greens. *"They are going galacking."*

galluses (n): suspenders.

gant (adj): lean, gaunt. *"The houses was bad ganted."*

gant-lot (n): pen for confining cattle during round-up.

gap (n): low spot in mountain range or between hills.

gaum; gom (v): to smear. *"His face was all gaumed up."*

gentle (v): to treat gently, to calm. *"See how he gentles the horse."*

get on (v): accuse, berate. *"She got on him about drinking."*

get shet of (v): dispose of. *"I got shet of that dog."*

ghostes (n): ghosts.

'gin (adv): before, by the time that. *"It'll be dark 'gin I get home."*

gip (n): female dog.

git-box or **git-fiddle** (n): guitar.

gitting-aroundest (adj): very active in the community. *"He's the gitting-aroundest man I ever seen."*

give out (v): (1) exhausted. *"I'm plumb give out."*
(2) decide against. *"I'm about give out going."*
(3) announce. *"It was give out there was to be a meeting last night."*

give up (v): to concede. *"He's give up to be the best doctor in town."*

good few (n): abundance. *"They's a good few apples this year."*

granny-trouble (n): birth. *"He had granny trouble at his house last night."*

granny-woman (n): midwife.

grave-rock (n): tombstone.

gravel (v): to annoy or embarass. *"That story always gravelled him."*

grinding rock (n): grindstone. *"He sharpened his axe on the grinding rock."*

gum (n): hive or container, as "bee gum" as made from hollow section of a gum tree.

H

hack (v): to annoy, embarrass. *"That story sure did hack him."*

hadn't orter (v): should not. *"He hadn't orter went."*

hain't (v): ain't. (am not, is not, are not, has not, have not)

ha'nt (n): ghost.

have (v): am, are, is. *"I have obliged to go."*

hear tell (v): hear or know. *"Did ye ever hear tell o' sich?"*

hecter (v): heckle. *"They allers like to hecter him."*

heifer (n): derogatory term for a woman. *"That's the ol' heifer that lives up the holler."*

helt (v): held. *"They helt on tight."*

hern (pn): hers.

het (v): heated. *"She het up the vittles."*

hez (v): has.

hickory (n): switch for punishment. *"If that young'un don't mind, I'll take a hickory to him."*

hippens (n): diapers.

his'n (pn): his. *"Hit's his'n."*

hisself (pn): himself.

hit (pn): it.

hog-meat (n): pork, generally fresh but some times cured.

hog wild (adj): wildly excited. *"She went hog wild when she hearn o' it."*

holler (n): hollow or ravine. *"They run down the holler."* (v): yell. *"I hollered fer him to come."*

holp (v): help. *"Hit holp a lot."*

hone (v): long for. *"He's honing fer a mess of hawg meat."*

hoof (v): walk. *"Them as ain't got horses'll have to hoof it."*

hot up (v): make warmer. *"Please hot up my coffee."*

hound dog (n): hound.

hull (n): cartridge. *"I had just two hulls fer my gun."*

hunkers (n): haunches. *"I set back on my hunkers."*

hurt fer (v): need. *"The house is* **hurting fer** *a coat of paint."*

hurting (n): pain. *"I had a powerful* **hurting** *in my chest."*

I

iffen or **effen** (conj): if. *"I'll come* **iffen** *I can."*

ile (n): oil. *"Bear's* **ile.**"

ill (adj; adv): evil, bad tempered. *"He's acting awful* **ill** *these days."*

improvement (n): a clearing in the woods, a house, etc., to enhance the value of property.

in a manner (adv): nearly. *"He's* **in a manner** *blind."*

ingern (n): onion.

innards (n): entrails. *"The bear clawed the dogs* **innards** *out."*

in reason (adv): beyond doubt. *"I knowed* **in reason** *he'd go."*

in this day and time (adv): now.

in time (adv): once. *"A house stood there* **in time."**

'ist (adv): just. *"Hit's* **'ist** *right."*

J

jag (n): a small amount. *"A* **jag** *o' corn."*

janders (n): jaundice. *"He's got yaller* **janders.**"

jedgematically (adv): in my judgment. **"Jedgematically,** *he'll come tomorrow."*

job (v): stab. *"He was* **jobbed** *with a knife."*

jower (v): quarrel. *"They'd been* **jowering** *for a long time."*

juberous (adj): dubious, doubtful. *"I was* **juberous** *of that all the time."*

jump-jacket (n): overall jacket.

K

keep (v): remain in session. *"Will school keep next week?"*

kernels (n): small glands in neck, armpits, groin, etc. These in some game animals must be removed if the meat is to be edible.

ketched, kotch or **kotched** (v): caught. *"We kotched two coons."*

kick (v): disparage. *"I ain't kicking his work none."*

kilt (n): killed. *"Who kilt that dog?"*

kinder, kindley (adv): rather. *"The road was kindley rough."*

kiver (v): cover. *"Hit was kivered with a board."* (n): quilt or blanket. *"Put another kiver on the bed."*

knock-fight (n): fist fight. *"Them boys had a big knock-fight."*

knowed (v): knew. *"I knowed it all the time."*

L

lamp oil (n): kerosene.

lap, tree lap (n): tree tops and limbs left on the ground after logging.

lastiest (adj): long lasting. *"Warnit (walnut) is the lastiest wood they is."*

lasty (adj): durable, lasting. *"Them was lasty britches."*

lavish (n): abundance. *"They was a lavish o' berries there."*

lay off to (v): intend. *"I laid off to go a long time ago."*

lay out (v): hide. *"They laid out in the woods 'til the law was gone."* (v): prepare for burial. *"Who laid out the corpse?"*

learn (v): teach. *"They didn't learn him to spell."*

least (adj): smallest, youngest. *"He's their least boy."*

leather britches (n): green beans dried in the shuck for winter use.

leave (v): let. *"Leave him go."*

led (n): lid. *"She broke the led to the pot."*

leesen (conj): unless. *"He'll come lessen he's sick."*

let on (v): pretend. *"She let on she wasn't goin'."*

lick (n): molasses. *"Give him some lick for his dodger."*

licking (n): whipping. *"Bud got a licking at school."*

light out (v): leave hurriedly, also *"light a shuck,"* *"light a rag."*

likeness (n): portrait or picture.

likeness taker (n): photographer. *"Be you the likeness taker?"*

little grain (n): small amount. *"Give me a little grain of licker."*

linkster (linquister) (n): interpreter.

long sweetning (n): sorghum molasees or syrup.

M

ma'ar (n): marrow. *"a* **ma'ar** *bone."*

main (adj): very, great. *"a* **main** *high mountain."*

make (v): produce. *"I'll* **make** *a good crop 'o corn."*

make out like (v): pretend. *"Jane* **made out like** *she was mad."*

manpower (v): to move some heavy object by human effort. *"We'll have to* **manpower** *them logs up."*

mast (n): acorns, chestnuts or beechnuts.

master (adj): great or fine. *"He's a* **master** *hand at hunting."*

meat (v): supply with meat. *"One hog will* **meat** *us all winter."*

meller (mellow) (v): beat. *"I'll* **meller** *his head if he pesters me."*

mend (v): improve physically. *"He's* **mending** *slowly."*

-ment (suffix): accented last syllable in such words as settlement', government', treatment', etc.

mess (n): lot, meal, etc. *"a* **mess** *o' beans."*

mighty (adv): very, exceedingly. *"He had some* **mighty** *big hogs."*

mind (v): remember. *"Don't you* **mind** *the day he came?"*
(v): care for. *"You* **mind** *the young'uns whilst I'm gone."*

misery (n): pain. *"I've got a* **misery** *in my stummick."*

mistook (v): mistaken or confused. *"I've been* **mistook** *about that lots of times."*

mizzling (adj): drizzle. *"They was a* **mizzling** *sort o' rain."*

molasses (n): sorghum syrup, always plural. *"Give me some o' them* **molasses.**"

mommick (v): to spoil or mess up. *"He* **mommicked** *everything."*

monstrous (adv): very. *"They killed a* **monstrous** *big bear."*

mostest (adj): most. *"Who growed the* **mostest** *corn?"*

most likely (adv): probably. *"***Most likely** *they'll be there."*

mottley (adj): mottled. *"The red cow had a* **mottley** *calf."*

mought (v): might. *"he* **mought** *go."*

much (v): pet, make over. *"He'll* **much** *a hound dog."*

muscle (v): lift by bodily strength. *"Hit took four men to muscle that rock up.*

N

na'ar (n): narrow. *"a na'ar bridge."*

name (v): mention. *"You name hit to paw."*

narrow-minded (adj): set in one's opinions. *"He's narrow-minded about a lot of things."*

nary (ne'er a) (pn): none, not any. *"Ain't nary one of 'em goin'."*

nary none (pn): not any. *"I ain't got nary none."*

necessaries (n): things needful. *"A feller has to carry his necessaries."*

needcessity (n): necessity.

neighbor (v): be neighborly with. *"They're fine folks to neighbor with."*

nestes (n): nests. *"birds' nestes."*

nigh onto (adv): nearly. *"Hit's nigh onto a mile."*

norate (v): to spread the news. *"Hit was norated all over the country."*

no sech (pn): not anything. *"I never said no sech."*

note (v): write music for. *"Can he note a song?"*

note up for (v): denote, indicate. *"Them colouds don't note up for rain."*

O

old man, old woman (n): husband, wife

on (prep): about. *"I'll think on it."*

oncet (adj): once.

onery or ornery (adj): mean, worthless. *"He's acting ornery these days."*

onliest (adj): only. *"Hit's the onliest knife I got."*

opine (v): judge, consider.

ourn (pn): ours. *"Them's ourn."*

outen (adj): out of. *"Put that dog outen the house."*

outlandish (adj): as opposed to *"foreignor"*, one from outside the mountains, *"outlandish"* refers to those from over seas.

overhauls (n): overalls. (pronunciation).

over yan (n): over there. *"They live over yan."*

own, own up to (v): acknowledge. *"He wouldn't own it as his'n." "John owned up to fighting."*

P

pack (v): carry. *"He packed all the corn home."*
(v): blame. *"Hit was all packed on him."*

painter (n): panther.

passel (n): parcel, group of people. *"They was a passel of folks at the meetin'."*

pay no mind (v): give no attention. **"Don't pay them no mind."**

peaked (adj): exhausted, ill. *"She looks peaked."*

peart (adj): well, lively. *"I'm feeling right peart."*

peartnin' powders (n): tonic, vitamins. *"Doc, John wants some more of those peartnin' powders that done him so good."*

peckerwood (n): woodpecker.

penitentiary (v): send to prison. *"They penitentiaried him for making licker."*

persackly (adv): exactly. *"She done persackly right."*

pester (v): bother, irritate. *"Don't pester the teacher."*

petered out (adj): exhausted. *"I was all petered out when I got there."*

peth (n): pith. *"Punch the peth outen that elder (alder) stick."*

phonographer (n): stenographer.

pieded (adj): spotted or mottled. *"A pieded calf."*

pilfering around (v): idly wandering, not necessarily to steal. *"Them boys were jest pilfering around."*

pintedly (pointedly) (adv): thoroughly. *"The big dog most pintedly whopped the other'ns."*

pint-blank (adv): directly, positively. *"I told 'em no--pint blank."*

pistol-gun (n): pistol

play (n): square dance.

play party (n): gathering where games were played and square dancing done.

pleasure (v): to give pleasure to or derive pleasure from. *"It pleasured him a lot to go."*

plumb (adv): very, completely. *"I'm just plumb wore out."*

19

plunder (n): household effects. *"They put all their **plunder** in one wagon."*

poke (n): small bag, usually paper. *"Put hit in a **poke**."*

pomper (n): pamper. *"Them young'uns is plumb **pompered**."*

pone (n): (1) a cake of bread. (2) swelling on the body, as a boil, abcess, tumor, etc.

pooch out (v): protrude. *"Hit's little belly was all **pooched out**."*

poorly (adv): ill, not well. *"I'm feeling purty **poorly**."*

poppet (n): doll. *"The least one was playing with hit's **poppet**."*

pop (n): skull, low grade illicit whiskey.

postes (n): posts. *"fence **postes**."*

poverty-poor (adj). destitute. *"That fambly (family) is plumb **poverty-poor**."*

powerful (adj): very. *"They cut down a **powerful** big tree."*

pretty (n): (1) play-pretty, toys, playthings.*"Pick up your play-**pretties**."* (2) something of value. *"I'd give a **pretty** to know."*

pretty-fying (v): making beautiful. *"She spent a time **pretty-fying** her face."*

projecting around (v): loitering, looking about. *"I've jest been **projectin' around**."*

prong (n): branch or fork of a stream. *"West **prong** of Little Pigeon River."*

proud (v): glad. *"I'm surely **proud** to see you."*

pummies (n): pomace, ground apples, peaches, etc. from which the juice had been pressed. *"After they made cider, they throwed the **pummies** on the ground."*

punying, punying around (v): not well, languid, etc. *"I've been **punying** around quite a spell."*

puny-like (adj): indisposed. *"The baby's been acting **puny-like**."*

purt' nigh (adv): almost, very close. *"I **purt' nigh** fell in."*

Q

quare (adj): queer. *"She always was a **quare** woman."*

quartering (adv): diagonally. *"He walked **quartering** across the field."*

quieten (v): to quiet. *"See if you can **quieten** him down."*

quiled (v): coiled. *"A big snake was **quiled** in the path."*

R

raise (v): rear. *"I was raised in the mountains."*

rations (n): food, either raw or prepared. *"Did he bring his rations with him?"*

red (v): arrange, make tidy. *"Set here while I red up the room."*

rench (v): rinse. *"Be shore to rench the clothes good."*

restes (v): rests. *"Wait while they restes."*

retch (v): pass or hand. *"I tol' him to retch me the shovel."*

revenuer (n): probation officer. *"Look out! The revenuer's comin'."*

rheumatiz (n): rheumatism. *"He's got the rheumatiz bad."*

rifle (n): gun, rifle.

right (adv): very. *"She was right sick."*

rightly (adv): correctly, justly. *"I can't rightly say."*

right smart (adj): a large quantity, very much, etc. *"I raised a right smart o' corn."*

rise (adv): in excess of. *"He had in the rise of 20 hogs."*

rising (n): boil, carbuncle. *"She had a rising on her neck."*

riz (v): raised. *"They all riz up."*

riz bread (n): risen or yeast bread.

rock (v): throw rocks at. *"Them boys rocked my house."*

roguish (adj): descriptive of a cow inclined to jump the fence or stray from the pasture.

roughness (n): fodder, food. *"I was gathering roughness for my stock."*

rosum (n): resin.

ruction (n): fight or riot. *"They was a turrible ruction at camp meeting."*

ruint (v): ruined. *"They ruint me."*

running set (n): square dance.

S

sallet (n): salad. *"Think I'll go out and pick me some **sallet** greens."*

sanging (v): digging ginseng (sang) root. *"We was **sanging** all day."*

sanginghoe (n): special implement for digging ginseng--narrow blade, short handle.

services (n): serviceberries or trees.

sashay (v): saunter or strut. *"He was **sashaying** around."*

sass (n): impudence. *"Don't give me none of your **sass**."*

sassy (adj): saucy. *"She talked awful **sassy**."*

scandalous (adj): very, exceedingly. *"Clothes costes **scandalous** high these days."*

scope (n): large tract of land. *"My brother heired a wide **scope** of land."*

scouting (v): hiding in woods or mountains to avoid capture by the law.

scringe (v): cringe. *"I seen him **scringe** when he heared it."*

seed (v): saw. *"I **seed** a monstrous big bear."*

set-along child (n): child big enough to sit on the floor but not walk.

settin' cheer (n): sitting chair, no rockers.

set into (v): begin. *"Hit **set into** raining about dark."*

setting upto (v): courting. *"Henry's **setting upto** the widder Brown."*

severe (adj): vicious. *"He's a terrible **severe** dog."*

shoe-mouth (adj): *"The snow was **shoe-mouth** deep."*

shoot (n): charges or loads, as *"two **shoots** of powder."*

shucky-beans (n): beans dried in the hull for winter use.

shumake (n): sumac.

's' I (v): said I. *"Your're crazy, **'s' I**."*

sich or sech (pn): such. *"I never said no **sech**."*

sideling (adj; adv): slanting, as a hillside. *"He planted his corn on **sideling** ground."*

sight (n): great deal much. *"They've had a **sight** o' trouble."*
(n) many. *"There was a **sight** o' people there."*

sing coarse (v): sing bass. *"He **sings coarse** at meeting."*

singlings (n): whiskey put through the still once, inferior to being run twice or put through a thumping chest.

skift (n): small amount. *"Jest a light **skift** of snow."*

slaunchwise (adj): diagonally, off a straight line. *"The fence come up the hill **slaunchwise**."*

slick, or laurel slick (n): rhododendron or kalmia thicket.

smidgen (n): small amount. *"Jest a **smidgen** more sugar in my coffee."*

snuck (v): sneaked. *"He **snuck** off when nobody was looking."*

sobby (adj): sodden. *"That field gets right **sobby** after a rain."*

some several (adj): goodly number. *"They was **some several** folks there."*

soon (adv): early. *"Come **soon** in the morning."*

soon start (n): early. *"They made a **soon start** this morning."*

sop (n): gravy.

sorgrums (n): sorghrum. Molasses made from locally grown cane. Always plural.

sorry (adj): poor, worthless. *"He bought a **sorry** sort of a horse."*

spang (adj; adv): various meanings, as directly, quickly, etc. (1) *"**spang**-fired new"*, (2) *"that dog jumped right **spang** into the creek."*

spark (v): court. *"Who's **sparking** her now?"*

spell (n): period of time. *"a long dry **spell**."*

spend an opinion (v): express one's idea. *"I wouldn't want to **spend an opinion** on that."*

sprangle (adj): spread out, like limbs of a tree. *"Laurel is a **sprangling** sort of bush."*

sprig (n): bit or particle, as *"a tiny **sprig** of fire."*

squander (v): scatter or wander idly. (1) *"Them little turkeys jest **squandered** around every which way."* (2) *"I jest **squandered** around all day."*

squinch owl (n): screech owl.

stand (n): hive of bees. *"Davis had nigh onto a hundred **stand** o' bees."*

start-nekked (adj): unclothed. *"They went swimming **start-nekked**."*

starved out (v): destitute. *"That family's just about **starved out**."*

still (v): to make illicit liquor. *"Is anybody stilling around here now?"*

stob (n): small stake or stub. *"He drove a stob in the ground."* (v): stab. *He was stobbed right in the heart."*

stomp (n): clearing with grass trodden of by horses or cattle. *"They's a big stomp on top of the mountain."*

store (v): to trade in a store. *"I've got a lot of storing to do."*

store-boughten (adj): purchased ready made, as *"store-boughten clothes."*

stout (adj): strong or well. *"I'm feeling purty stout."*

strut (v): swell. *"My fingers was all strutted out."*

sugar tree (n): hard maple, from whose sap maple sugar is made.

sull (v): to act sullen, feign death. *"A 'possum'll sull when a dog ketches it."*

sunup (n): **sundown** (n): sunrise, sunset.

surround (v): go around. *"We surrounded the hill."*

survigorous (adj): vicious, exceedingly strong. *"Hit was a powerful survigorous bear."*

swag (n): low spot in the ground, on a ridge.

sweetening (n): (1) short sweetening - sugar. (2) long sweetening - syrup, molasses.

sweet talk (v): flattery. *"Don't sweet talk me."*

swolt (v): swelled. *"His face was all swole up."*

T

tacky (adj): shabby, out of style. *"That hat is sortor **tacky**."*

tad (n): small amount. *"Jest a **tad** more sugar, please."*

tain't (v): it isn't. *"**Tain't** what I wanted."*

taken (v): took. *"I **taken** the gun."*

take off (v): leave hurriedly. *"He **taken off** down the road."*

take up (v): begin. *"Has meeting **took up** yet?"*

talking to (v): courting. *"Jim's been **talking to** Arminty nigh onto three years."*

task (v): to assign duty. *"Ye can't **task** a man that way."*

tastes (2 syllables) (v): *"Hit **tastes** sorter bitter."*

tell 'tother from which (adj): distinguish between. *"Them young'uns was so like I couldn't **tell 'tother from which**."*

tetched (adj): feeble-minded or slightly deranged. *"Their least boy is sorter **tetched**."*

tetchous (adj): irritable. *"She's powerful **tetchous** these days."*

tetotally (adv): totally, completely. *"I'm most **tetotally** wore out."*

textes (n): texts.

thar (adj): pronunciation of *"there"*.

that 'air (that there) (adj): that. *"He went through **that 'air** door."*

theirn (pn): theirs. *"Is hit **theirn?**"*

they (pn): there. *"**They** was two men there."*

thickness (n): *"about the **thickness** of a dollar."*

thoughen (conj): unless, without. (1) *"He won't go **thoughen** they call him."* (2) *"She made bread **thoughen** any salt."*

thoughty (adj): thoughtful. *"That was mighty **thoughty** of you."*

thumping chest, key or (simply) **thumper** (n): a part of a whiskey still, between the boiler and the condenser.

thunder gust (n): electrical storm.

tide (n): flood or freshet. *"They was a awful high **tide** in the river last Spring."*

'til (prop): until. *"They stayed **'til** dark."*

time about (adv): alternately. *"They go to her church and his'n,* **time about.***"*

toddick (n): small measuring vessel used in taking toll at a grist mill, hence-small amount.

tolable (adj): tolerable. *"Air ye feelin'* **tolable?"**

tole (v): entice, lure. *"They took some corn to* **tole** *the turkeys in."*

took down or took down sick (v): sick abed. *"Henry was* **took down** *last week."*

tooken (v): taken. *"The ham was* **tooken** *out of my smokehouse."*

took up (v): arrested. *"John was* **took up** *fer stealing corn."*

tooth bresh (n): twig with one end chewed into a rude brush, used in dipping snuff.

tooth-dentist or tooth doctor (n): dentist.

torn-downdest (adj): delapidated, messed up, etc. *"That's the* **torn-downdest** *house I ever seen."*

tote (v): carry. *"How much can you* **tote?***"*

tote fair (v): deal honestly. *He'll* **tote fair** *in a trade."*

tother (n): the other. *"I seen him* **tother** *day."*

tow sack (n): burlap bag.

tree (v): cause to take refuge in a tree. *"My dogs* **treed** *a monstrous big coon."*

tree-dog (n): dog trained to tree game.

tree lap or simply **lap** (n): tops and limbs of trees on the ground after logging.

tree sugar (n): sugar made by boiling down the sweet sap of hard maple tree. Also called tree syrup and tree molasses.

trinkle (v): trickle. *"The water comes* **trinkling** *out of the rock."*

tromp (v): tramp. *"Them horses* **tromped** *down the wheat."*

tuckered out (adj): exhausted. *"I'm plumb* **tuckered out.***"*

turn out (v): dismiss. *"Has school* **turned out** *yet?"*

tushes (n): tusks, as of hog or bear.

twarn't (v): it was not. *'***Twarn't** *so."*

27

U

unbeknowst (adj): without notice or warning. *"He left **unbeknowst** to anybody."*

up an' done (v): immediately. *"He **up an' done** it."*

use (v): live in or frequent. *"Bears **use** along that ridge."*

V

varmint (n): almost any wild animal.

vex (v): annoy. *"Them young'uns **vexed** him terrible."*

vigrus (adj): vigorous. *"He's plumb **vigrus** these days."*

vittles (n): food.

vomick (v): vomit.

W

wait on (v): court, woo. *"John's **waitin'** on that new gal."*

was a week (year) ago (adv): last week. *"He was here, **was a week** ago."*

waspes or waspers (n): wasps.

wax (n): chewing gum.

way off (adv): remote, far. *"They come from **way off**."*

wear out (v): to flog or whip. *"She **wore** that young'un plumb **out**."*

weasley (adj): wizened. *"Looks sorter **weasley**, don't he?"*

we'uns (pn): we, us. *"Are **we'uns** goin'?"*

whar (adv): pronunciation of 'where'.

whelps (n): welts. *"The whuppin' raised great **whelps** on his back."*

whetrock (n): whetstone.

whilst (conj): while. *"Eat some vittles **whilst** you wait."*

whup (v): whip. *"Who **whupped**?"*

whur (adv): whether. *"I don't know **whur** to go or not."*

widder-man (n): widower.

widder-woman (n): widow.

wind-throwed (adj): blown over by wind. *"All the big trees was **wind throwed**."*

windy (n): a tall tale. *"Look out or them fellers'll tell you a **windy**."*

wish book (n): catalog of mail order house.

withouten (conj): without, unless. *"I won't go **withouten** you do."*

women folks (n): women. *"The **women folks** had all gone to meeting."*

woods colt (n): illegitimate child.

woolly patches or woollies (n): rhododendron thickets.

work-brittle (adj): industrious.

worn out (adj): tired or exhausted. *"I was just all **worn out**."*

writing (n): something written, a letter, etc. *"They give him a **writin'** to take to the judge."*

Y

yan or **overyan** (adv): yonder. *"They live **overyan** in Tennessee."*

yarb (n): herb.

yarb doctor (n): one (untrained) who treats illnesses with herbs, roots, etc.

years (n): ears.

yearth (n): earth.

yo (n): ewe, female sheep.

you-all (pn): sometimes heard in mountain speech, but regarded as intrusion from Deep South.

yourn (pn): yours. *"Hits's all **yourn**."*

youernses (pn): your. *"Who was over at **youernses** house?"*

you-uns (pn): you. *"Can **you-uns** come?"*

MISCELLANEOUS

Quadruple negative:
"I ain't never seen no sech thing, nohow."

Threat of an old lady, "pestered" by some boys:
"If I hear nary 'nother word out of ary one of you'uns, I'll take me a bresh and most pintedly frail hell out'n the whole passel o' you'-un."

Man telling of seeing his dog swept away by a swollen stream:
"When I last seen him, he were, as you mought say, a-dealing of his feet and a-doing of no good."

"Me and a passel more gals was comin' over t'mar-r to have our likenesses struck, an' we'll be shorely disappinted."

"I don't care" gives assent. "Will you have some of the ham?"
"I don't care," or "I don't care if I do."

"The onliest way he knowed to get rid o' that tooth was to jump it out." Placing a nail against the tooth at its root and striking the nail with a smart blow.

"I never had no trouble with my teeth. They just rotted out naturally."

"Hit don't seem right for a feller to be workin' when they's a death in the neighborhood."

"Maw, give Shorty some lick. He wants to wallup his dodger."
(Put syrup on his corn bread.)

"We all wanted to be at meetin', but John - he took the studs and wouldn't go."

PAUL M. FINK was a well-known local historian from Washington County, Tennessee, where he served as the official historian for much of his life. He served as vice president of the Tennessee Historical Society, the Tennessee Archaeological Society, and the Tennessee Folklore Society. He was a leader in the movement that led to the establishment of the Great Smoky Mountains National Park. Working with George Masa and others, he was largely responsible for routing the Appalachian Trail through the Great Smokies and nearby mountain ranges. Fink was an active leader in the Appalachian Trail Conference, serving on its Board from 1925 to 1949, and was the author of *Backpacking Was the Only Way*, an account of early twentieth century camping and backpacking adventures in the southern Appalachians.

CPSIA information can be obtained
at www.ICGtesting.com
Printed in the USA
LVOW12s2038060218
565506LV00002B/214/P